GARDEN
LOVE

GARDEN LOVE

Plants   Dogs

Country Gardens   **Simon Griffiths**

 Thames & Hudson

Contents

Introduction

Meadowbank at the start of spring, with the prunus trees in full blossom.

TOP Meadowbank. **BOTTOM** A collection of Victorian photographs showing the first family to live in the cottage.

I don't know how it happened, but
one day I woke up and found myself living
in the inner suburbs, in a boring house with a tiny
garden. Feeling dissatisfied with city life, my partner, Ian,
and I decided it was time for a change. We started looking for
a place in the country almost straight away. The brief was simple:
a small house with a decent-sized garden—not so big that we would
become slaves to the garden, but with room for some trees, a few beds
of perennials and a shed.

The second house we looked at, we bought. The property is in Kyneton,
an hour out of Melbourne, about halfway to Bendigo and the goldfields.
It's not the outback, but it's far enough out of town to feel you are in the
country. Meadowbank, as it's known, is a simple Georgian cottage, built
in the 1850s by a Scottish master stonemason, Alexander Rodger,
who lived here with his wife and eleven children. It is a small, neat,
brick and bluestone cottage, the kind of house that looks like a child's
drawing: a door in the middle with a window either side, a hipped roof
and a chimney with smoke drifting out of it. The house is situated on
the front boundary and when we moved in the large backyard was
a blank canvas just waiting for a garden.

When we first arrived, the area was in the middle of a drought and
the yard looked like a dust bowl—even the copious weeds were all dead.
A rusty Hills hoist was just about the only thing still standing, along
with some dead silver birch trees and a big old cedar (*Cedrus deodara*).
We first set about improving the soil: digging in truckloads of mushroom
compost, buckets of manure from a neighbour and coffee grounds from
a local café. Turning over the old soil was like an archaeological dig, as
we uncovered decades of buried rubbish: shards of antique blue and
white china, bottles of all descriptions, dozens of glass marbles,
bicycle parts, old boots, coins, doorknobs, brooches and
enough clock parts to build several clocks. (Still to
this day, the strangest things turn up.)

We knew from the outset that we
wanted to create a double perennial border,
so, after giving the house a hasty coat of paint, we dove
headlong into planting. We already knew a bit about the local
climate, but the conditions proved to be even more challenging
than we had prepared ourselves for. Gardening in this region of
Australia comes with unique problems: scorching summer temperatures,
drought and bushfires, not to mention snakes and rabbits. In addition, the
winter frosts are surprisingly heavy. We soon discovered that even supposedly
frost-hardy plants have a habit of curling up their toes after the first bite of
winter. Into the bargain, it turns out the soil in our part of Kyneton is heavy
black pug, which sets like concrete in summer and is too sticky to work in winter.
The combination of frost and wet feet is doubly deadly and, despite our efforts to
improve the soil and drainage, we lost much of what we planted in the first year.
Rather than be disheartened, the lesson I took away from that false start is that
every garden is unique. Learning the ins and outs of different gardens and
locales is all part of a gardener's life-long education; we never stop growing
our knowledge of climate, soil, plants and life cycles. And that is a big part
of the joy of it.

After a little time, we began a more systematic trial-and-error gardening
style at Meadowbank. Now and again a neighbour—let's call her Mrs M—
would stick her head over the fence, point a bony finger at something and
say, 'That looks frost tender, it will be dead in a few weeks!' Considering
Mrs M lived in a tiny cottage whose garden contained three rose bushes and
an apple tree, with a husband who spent his spare time poisoning anything
else that dared to poke a green shoot out of the earth, we took her advice with
a grain of salt. Under Mrs M's watchful eye (or more likely, despite it) we started
to learn what would grow in the climate and soil. I had envisaged large drifts
of Mediterranean echiums, rosemary and lavender, with swarms of happy bees
in summer, but such a dream was not to be: soggy feet and heavy frosts soon
finished them off.

Driving around the area was a great way to get fresh inspiration.
The locals were successfully growing buddleias, lilacs, roses, clematis,
irises and poppies. Lamb's ear (*Stachys byzantine*), we soon learned,
is so comfortable growing in Kyneton conditions that it self-sows
and can be found in almost every garden. Over time, we have
learned which plants will grow in our soil, don't mind
wet feet over winter and can cope with the
extremes in climate.

In spring, the summerhouse is quickly engulfed by a Lamarque climbing rose.

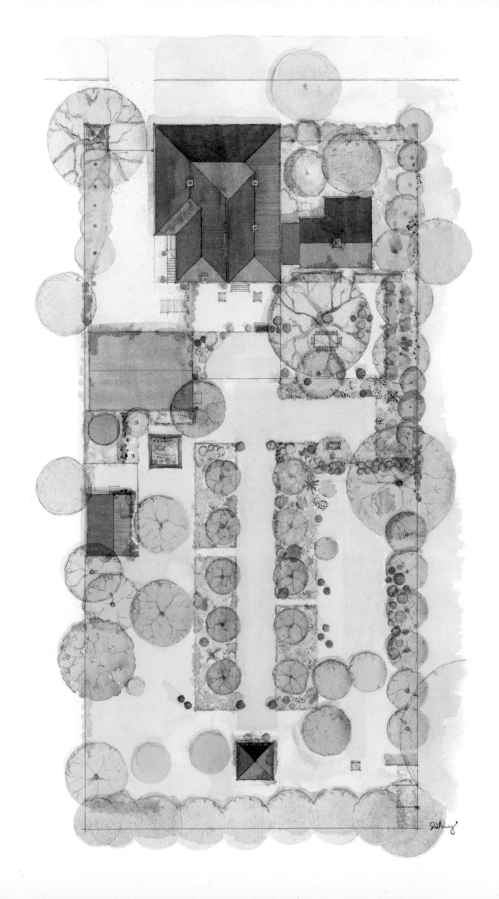

Nowadays, the garden
feels like it's thriving. Burgeoning
trees, hedges and other plantings give the space
a sense of being divided into numerous 'rooms'. Various
grasses give the garden a soft billowy feel for much of the
year and look beautiful when backlit in the evening light. Topiary
balls of box, on the other hand, act as punctuation marks, breaking up
the garden and providing some form to look at in winter when the rest of
the garden is asleep. Dahlias add a refreshing splash of colour, while smaller
treasures like snowdrops and cyclamen, which multiply rapidly in our climate,
spill from their pots and self-sow in unexpected spots around the garden.

We are lucky to live in a part of the world where there are four distinct seasons, each
magical in its own way. In winter, when the garden is bare, the frosts dust everything
with icing sugar, the grass is crunchy underfoot, and water in the stone troughs
freezes over for days at a time. In spring, you can feel the warmth in the soil as
you weed the garden beds, shoots and buds burst to life and bulbs spring up to
brighten odd corners of the garden. In summer, the garden is brimming, with
not a patch of bare soil to be seen. Warm evenings and long days mean it is
possible to live in the garden. We often drag an old Persian rug onto the grass
and sit and enjoy a gin and tonic while we discuss plans for new plantings or
what changes to make to the borders for next year. Our two whippets, Frederico
and Umberto, frolic on the lawn. The atmosphere shifts in autumn: things are
quieter, the garden contemplative. The business of summer is done and the
garden starts to feel sleepy. This is when the light is at its most beautiful.
Slowly plants unwind: the grasses dry out and change to blonde, the dahlias
come into their own and there is another flush of roses. We tidy away dead
plants, giving others the chance to show their forms and colours.

Self-seeders have become a big part of the garden. I love the unpredictable
way some plants creep their way around the beds or escape them completely,
softening any formality the garden has. Every year is different in a garden like
this. Some years we have masses of poppies, others just a few. Queen Anne's lace
moves around the garden under its own steam, appearing and disappearing
seemingly at will. The population of triffid-like cardoons (*Cynara cardunculus*)
is also on the move: some years they are at the front of a border, some years
at the back, while other times they pop up in a different part of the garden
altogether. Successful self-seeders in our garden include: lamb's ear,
Verbena bonariensis, verbascums of various sorts, fennel, borage
and *Cerinthe major*—along with a few things that I've been
gifted that I don't even know the names of.

A watercolour painting of the
Meadowbank garden by my partner, Ian.

Behind the vegetable patch, Ian's shingled studio is made almost entirely of recycled materials.

In spring,
the borders
fill out quickly to
become a wild tapestry
of colour and texture,
while buxus balls
add a formal
element.

As we continued on
our gardening adventure, we started
to make gardening friends. You may not be
aware that there is a secret gardening network in this
country! People with great gardens know other people with
great gardens, and securing an invitation to visit is usually a simple
matter of asking to be introduced. This, for me, has been the best part
of moving to the country and creating my own garden—meeting all these
amazing gardeners and getting to see their private gardens. To me, the real
beauty of gardens is that they reflect an extension of an individual's life
and personality.

Through the 'secret' gardening network, I've had the privilege of visiting lots
of gorgeous gardens and spending time with their fascinating owners. Like the
gardens they create, gardeners come in a diverse range of shapes and sizes.
There are the plant collectors, so badly bitten by the gardening bug that they
will beg, borrow and even steal the plants they desire. The vegetable growers,
who eye each square foot of ground as precious productive soil and view
ornamental plants as a waste of space—proudly posting to Instagram each
bunch of carrots and bowl of berries they harvest. The romantics, who create
landscapes of pure beauty, their houses surrounded by a shimmering haze of
flowering plants, bees and butterflies. The design lovers, who combine straight
lines, mass plantings and clipped hedges to create the 'perfect' look. The native
plant enthusiasts, who can't bear to have an exotic plant in their Australiana
oasis. The thrifty gardeners who, as a point of honour, refuse to buy plants
and instead propagate their own from divisions and cuttings. And the larger-
than-life characters with gardens to match, their grand-scale gardens getting
bigger and bigger each year as they put in plants by the hundreds.

I find visiting these gardens and meeting their owners to be so inspiring.
I never fail to take away an idea I'll be able to use in my own garden; whether
a planting scheme, a combination of colours, a particular design element or a
contrast of textures or materials. Many of the gardens featured here are open
to the public—either periodically or permanently—and I highly recommend
you visit them if you can. Strolling through incredible gardens like these is
an invaluable way to learn about plants and gardening: you can observe
how big certain plants get, when different species bloom, how a
particular combination of plants might work together, how the
gardener manages the plants through the seasons and,
of course, discover new and interesting varieties.

TOP The summerhouse soon after it was completed (before it was
covered by rambling roses and white wisteria). BOTTOM A small
gate built from garden stakes and flanked by an informal hedge of
box balls helps define different spaces in the garden.

A vase of silver foliage picked from the garden.

Ian enjoys a glass of wine in the late-afternoon sunshine.

Freddy and Berto enjoying the garden.

A mixed bunch of red dahlias. I started by buying red Mrs Rees dahlias but have since collected many more varieties.

Most garden owners
are very happy to share their
knowledge and more often than not a polite
request for a cutting or some seeds is answered
with the quick snip snip of secateurs, the passing over
of a brown paper bag of seeds, or the digging up of a clump
of something special. It's through such generosity that I have
been lucky enough to obtain many wonderful specimens that are
rare or have perhaps gone out of fashion and are impossible to buy in
a nursery. One of my favourite garden people recently gave me a leaf off
her prize begonia, a truly beautiful plant and one that I have never seen
anywhere else. I have been able to propagate this treasure thanks to the
secret network and was glad to be able to return the favour by sending
her some seeds of *Cerinthe major*, which she was keen to try in her own
garden. I have acquired so many plants this way and when I look around
my garden I am reminded of all the gardens and gardeners that have
shaped it. The huge cluster of cardoons that has colonised the back
of one border grew from a few seeds Susan Irvine gave me years
ago. Flanders poppies, grown from seeds gifted to me by another
gardening friend, come up year after year without fail and
remind me of her beautiful garden.

A while ago I bought an old copy of a Gertrude Jekyll gardening
book. Pressed between the pages I discovered a small handwritten
note from the great lady herself, to a garden owner who had requested
some seeds from her garden at Munstead Wood. I can just imagine his
excitement at receiving this letter, with some Himalayan blue poppy
seeds tucked inside the folds. This scribbled message, a small act of
kindness from one passionate gardener to another, is one of my most
prized mementos. It shows that the secret network has been around for
a very long time.

It's been a great joy and privilege to become part of the gardening
'club', to get to explore so many remarkable gardens and also to
have people visit and enjoy the garden I have created. Every
great garden evokes a particular mood or atmosphere and
it can be hard to put your finger on exactly how or
why it achieves this—it's this unique quality
I try to capture in my photographs.

TOP LEFT The Gertrude Jekyll letter. **TOP RIGHT** Peonies: a present from Michelle and Cliff, grown in their garden at Foss. **BOTTOM LEFT** Gardening essentials. **BOTTOM RIGHT** Snowdrops (*Galanthus elwesii*) love our cold winters.

Introduction / 19

Silhouettes: grasses in the borders provide form and texture during the winter months.

Alowyn

An early morning bird's-eye view of the parterre garden at Alowyn.

The thing I love
most about visiting gardens like
Alowyn, which are open to the public,
is that I learn so much from them. Plants are
labelled and you can gain detailed knowledge of
different varieties before you commit to growing the plants
yourself. You can observe how big something grows, how it
works with other plants in the garden, how long its flowering
period is and how it changes from season to season. Alowyn gardens
and nursery in the Yarra Valley was set up with just this intention: to
provide information and to educate gardeners.

Commenced in 1997, the gardens cover 1.5 hectares (4 acres) and are
divided into five main areas: the perennial border, a formal parterre
garden, a silver birch forest, an edible garden with masses of fruit trees,
and display gardens. For me, the perennial border is the clear standout.
An Australian version of the classic English perennial border, it's
been created with plant varieties that suit the Victorian climate.
A sinuous path winds through the border and plants spill out onto
it from the un-edged beds. The relaxed atmosphere feels effortless,
but a lot of thought and planning has gone into creating the border:
the plants need to withstand temperatures ranging from −5 to 42
degrees Celsius and be able to survive periods of dry in summer.

The border is a riot of colour, texture and form from early spring
through to late autumn, the display changing weekly as different
plants come into flower. The plants graduate from low-growing
varieties at the front of the borders to tall ones at the back—although
here and there a tall plant is used to create some drama up the front,
or has been allowed to grow out onto the path so you have to push by
it on your way past. The border includes: salvias, sedums, verbascum,
phormium, grasses, succulents, penstemon, echinacea and Russian sage.

It takes a lot of work to get a perennial border looking this good:
ensuring the plants work with their neighbours, that the colours
complement each other and that the textures of the foliage,
flowers and seed heads all sit together in a harmonious way.
Winter, when the plants are dormant, is used as a time
to 'edit' the border; dividing plants and creating
new combinations. A perennial border is a
constant work in progress.

The first rays of sunlight hit a sundial in the perennial border.

My favourite part of the garden: the informal double border with path
snaking through, perennials spilling over and softening the edges.

The antique sundial sits at the centre of the garden.

The sundial is surrounded by billowing masses of *Sedum* 'Autumn Joy' and phormium.

TOP View through the borders to the grapevine-covered hills of the Yarra Valley.
BOTTOM LEFT Red amaranth. BOTTOM RIGHT Rosehips at the end of autumn.

The amazing
tapestry of
Attila's garden.

Attila's Garden

When Attila Kapitany
and his wife, Michele, purchased this
1-acre block on the outskirts of Melbourne, the
surrounding area was all farmland. The north-facing
property is within a green belt, so the garden looks out over
open green parkland, and a view of the original farm dam is part
of the borrowed landscape. Echidnas and wedge-tailed eagles visit
the garden, and the area has plenty of kangaroos. A boundary hedge of
conifers (*Cupressocyparis leylandii* 'Castlewellan Gold') protects the garden
from winds and provides a degree of privacy—though two 'portholes' cut
into the hedge give curious passers-by a glimpse of what lies beyond.

Attila specialises in succulents. Having written and illustrated more than
seven books on the subject, he is Australia's pre-eminent succulent expert.
He is a passionate champion for the use of succulents in Australian
gardens and his own garden is filled with all manner of these drought-
tolerant plants, including agaves, yuccas, bottle trees and Australian
natives, most of which have been grown from seed and
propagated by Attila and Michele.

This is a garden brimming with colour, texture and
form all year round. Succulents have great shape
and structure even when they're not flowering.
When they are in bloom, the garden is an oasis
of pure saturated colour, the air filled with the
buzzing of thousands of bees. The garden is divided into
'rooms', with gravel and sand paths meandering through
and steps made from local rock. The areas have different
microclimates, which Attila uses to full effect by growing a variety
of succulents that each require specific conditions to thrive. One of
the rooms, referred to as 'The Ruins', boasts stacks of angular basalt
stones, dug from the hillside and piled into tall towers.

Atilla grows eight different species of brachychiton or bottle
tree — a genus you don't see in a lot of Victorian gardens. He also
cultivates the impressive Gymea lily (*Doryanthes excelsa*), which
can grow up to 4 metres in height, each enormous prehistoric-
looking spike supporting a bunch of red flowers. The mix of
plants in this garden is completely individual, just like
the owners themselves.

The bare branches of a silk floss tree (*Ceiba speciosa*), amid copious
flowering succulents: pink and red Lampranthus, yellow *Aeonium
arboreum* flowers, silver-white Cotyledon orbiculata 'Silver Waves',
with blue patches of *Senecio mandraliscae*.

The spectacular rock formations created by Attila and Michele are one of the highlights of the garden.

The garden is a mix of succulents, agave, cacti—all expertly art-directed by Attila.

TOP LEFT Luminous pink and purple sedums, also known as house leeks.
TOP RIGHT Pink Lampranthus. **BOTTOM LEFT** African daisy (*Gazania*)
BOTTOM RIGHT *Aeonium arboreum*

An area of granitic sand creates a desert micro-climate in the garden.

Pink and red lampranthus and yellow *Aeonium arboreum* flowers add splashes of colour among the rock towers. In the background are the bare branches of a silk floss tree (*Ceiba speciosa*).

TOP LEFT *Senecio mandraliscae* **TOP RIGHT** Red lampranthus
BOTTOM LEFT Yucca filamentosa **BOTTOM RIGHT** Agave americana

View over
the urn garden
and out across
the Tarago
Reservoir.

Broughton Hall

The otherworldly
cries of peacocks fill the air as you
enter the gate to Broughton Hall, in the
tiny town of Jindivick. The long, curved drive leads
you through a large wooded area, the peacocks swishing
between the ghostly trunks of silver birch trees (*Betula
pendula*). Without warning, a set of ornate gates appears, marking
the entry to the house and formal garden.

When David Musker and his partner, Phillip Hunter, found this site in
1996 it was just a cow paddock, but as soon as they saw the location, they
were sold. For a start, the property has the most incredible, heart-stopping
views of the Tarago Reservoir. Secondly, this area of southern Victoria has
deep, rich soil and excellent rainfall, perfect for gardening.

From the rear of the house, a series of terraces spill down the hill.
The top terrace is quite formal, the buxus hedges clipped with knife-edge
precision and the beds overflowing with flowering perennials and large
silver cardoons. As the terraces move down the slope, they become
gradually less formal. David has included interesting architectural
elements throughout: one terrace has a double row of columns swathed
in climbing roses, another features enormous urns resting on a luxuriant
bed of lavender. Wherever you are standing, though, there are always
the magnificent vistas out over the reservoir.

Over the years, David has filled the garden with hundreds of unusual
and rare plants. These are his passion and in fact he runs a nursery in
town that specialises in such plants. Hedges and shrubs have been cleverly
used to enclose and create microclimates. There are more than 1000 roses,
many of them old-fashioned varieties and all of them flourishing. A central
pathway acts as the backbone of the garden, but there are other smaller
paths you can use to explore. Wandering through, you'll probably catch
the odd glimpse of David and Phillip's Highland cattle in the verdant
paddocks beyond the garden.

Everything here is lush and thriving, thanks in part to the climate
and soil, but also because David mulches heavily and the
plants respond. The archways and arbours dripping with
roses smothered in perfect blooms are enough to
make even the toughest gardener envious.

Crepuscule roses clamber over one of the garden's many arches.

A view over the more formal part of the garden, with the reservoir in the background. Chunky box hedges keep the masses of plantings in their beds.

In the column garden, climbing roses are underplanted with valerian (*Centranthus ruber* 'Alba').

TOP Morning light over one of the parterres.
BOTTOM A moss-encrusted bench in the silver birch wood.

TOP Another parterre, with pink and red valerian spilling over the box hedges.
BOTTOM A Lutyens bench in one of the areas leading into the rose gardens.

Broughton Hall / 53

One of David's peacocks promenading through the silver birch forest.

TOP LEFT Early morning light illuminates a big patch of valerian.
TOP RIGHT David's poodle, Merlin. **BOTTOM** The garden is famous
for its plantings of roses.

Cloudehill

Autumn is
the best time
of year to visit
Cloudehill.

It is hard to believe
the creator of Cloudehill gardens,
Jeremy Francis, used to be a wheat farmer in
arid Western Australia. His old life couldn't be more
removed from his current one, living and gardening at an
elevation of 580 metres in the temperate Dandenong Ranges,
where the deep volcanic loam soil receives an average rainfall of 1.25
metres a year.

Jeremy and his wife, Val, bought the former Woolrich flower farm and
nursery in the early 1990s with the goal of creating their dream garden.
The property had good bones, with magnificent established trees including
European beech, tri-colour beech, weeping Japanese maples and numerous
hedges, but it still took six months of solid clearing to remove the many
weed trees and tenacious blackberries. Only then could they begin to
create their garden.

Cloudehill is divided into a number of garden 'rooms' arranged along a
central axis. Beginning at 'The Water Garden', you pass down some brick
steps to 'The Warm Borders', a large room of hot-coloured red, orange
and yellow flowering perennials. This leads on to 'The Maple Court',
home to a pair of imperial Japanese maples that were imported from
the famous Yokohama Nursery Company in 1928. Further along the axis
is 'The Cool Borders', with plantings of cool-coloured perennials in silver,
blue and softer pastel tones. At the very end of the axis is 'The Summer
House Garden', where an Arts and Crafts–style brick summerhouse
shelters under the branches of an enkianthus tree (*E. campanulatus*).

Autumn is my favourite time to visit Cloudehill. The garden is full of
colour, as the deciduous trees and plants put on their final show before
winter, while blonde, fluffy grasses provide a contrasting softness.
The perennial borders have an overblown beauty, full of seed heads
and berries. The physical volume of the plantings throughout
the garden works to temper the hard surfaces of the walls,
arches and paved paths, creating a wonderful balance
of form and texture.

The garden is full of mature and historic trees.

The resplendent Japanese maples.

At the peak of autumn the garden is full to bursting with the contrasting colours and textures of leaves, seed heads and berries.

A path along the central axis leads from 'The Warm Borders' to 'The Cool Borders'.

A large Italian terracotta urn draws the eye and leads you further into the garden.

Autumn seed heads and berries are, in their own way, just as beautiful as flowers.

The garden contains many sculptures: a mix of classical figures and 21st century letter cutting. **BOTTOM RIGHT** A piece by artist and letter cutter Ian Marr.

A Victorian glazed ceramic garden bench.

Rosehips.

Westringia fruticosa balls contrast with local eucalypts to create an exciting entrance to the garden.

Flinders Garden

This Mornington
Peninsula garden was created
by landscape designer Ben Scott as a
coastal retreat for a busy Melbourne family.
The garden is elegant in its simplicity. It has
an almost Japanese feel in its handling of form and
structure, created by Ben's clever repetition of spheres
and use of striking colour contrasts throughout.

On driving into the secluded property, you are met by a forest
of narrow-leaved peppermint gums (*Eucalyptus radiata*), a sleek,
black guesthouse crouching between the trees. Behind a chunky
post-and-rail fence, the low-slung main house hugs the contours
of the land. Against the dark-coloured walls, the plantings
have been kept simple yet sculptural. A veritable army of
tightly clipped coastal rosemary (*Westringia fruticosa*) and
teucrium (*T. fruticans*) stand guard, while flowering
acanthus (*A. mollis*) shoot up their architectural
spires of blooms in front of one of the larger
windows. Here, at the front of the house,
the bucolic views out to the surrounding
farmland and bushland are equally
as important as the plantings.

Stepping stones lead to a large gravel forecourt
planted with graceful maples (*Acer*). To the left of the
house are some neat raised garden beds where the family
grows vegetables, herbs and flowers for cutting. The pool
area is hedged with Portuguese laurel (*Prunus lusitanica*) and
at the far end is a fire pit area: a gravelled rectangle planted
with four ginkgo trees that will eventually form a shady
canopy over the space. Seating has been created out of
massive square sections of timber beams, adding to
the sculptural, graphic feel that carries through the
garden. A lush lawn leads to the rear of the house,
where stands of white-trunked silver birch
trees form a stark contrast against
the dark walls.

Westringia balls and copper-coloured *Carex comans*
'Bronze Curls' in formation, with a few teucriums thrown in.

The pool, bordered with Portuguese laurel.

Paving stones set into the lawn create a simple but effective pathway.

The box balls provide a suitable modern landscape for the house.

A swathe
of carex grass
and topiary balls
surround a
lawned area.

TOP Planter boxes hold vegetables and flowers for the house, including pink and red sweet peas.
BOTTOM Restrained plantings of silver birch stand out against the dark exterior of house.

TOP Architectural hedges of English box and Portuguese laurel.
BOTTOM A simple palette of plants has been used to edge the tennis court.

Foss

Looking out across the paddocks on a frosty morning at Foss, with the Manchurian pears in full colour.

Crouched in a little
hollow on a bend of the Campaspe
River, at Green Hill in central Victoria, is Foss.
Belonging to Michelle Hylan and Cliff Pannam, Foss
has a huge sense of place and a large dose of magic. The
garden and house were constructed by the previous owners,
artists Peter and Helen Cole, but Michelle has cleverly tweaked what
they made to absolutely make the place her own.

The approach to the house offers a wonderful view over the property. Rock
walls and old cypresses stand like a series of exclamation marks in the blonde
grass of the paddocks that surround the garden. Manchurian pears line the
driveway up to the house, which has been built around an old bluestone
cottage. Along the front of the house is a fenced topiary garden, the buxus
painstakingly clipped into shape by Michelle.

Summers here are hot and dry, so the garden is not so large that it
can't be watered throughout the warmer months. It also includes lots
of hardy drought-tolerant plants, such as Portuguese laurel (*Prunus
lusitania*), olive trees and established hawthorns. Winters can be quite
harsh as well, with temperatures down to −5 degrees Celsius. This suits
the cold-loving peonies and hydrangeas, but in summer Michelle has to
cover them with sheets to protect them from the hot sun. From one
of the bedrooms, you can spy a beautiful hidden vista: a terracotta oil
jar underplanted with thick clumps of snowdrops, which thrive in the
conditions at Foss.

The rear garden feels very Mediterranean. The swimming pool enclosure has
a small patch of luxuriant lawn shaded by a large fig tree and a superb quince.
Nearby are beds of flowers for cutting and vegetables. Behind this, a formal
rectangle of plane trees forms the main view from the back of the house.
Looking further beyond, over the surrounding rocky paddocks, you could
be forgiven for thinking you were in Sicily.

A short walk from the house is the river, lined with ancient
eucalypts that hang out over the water. The river feels almost
part of the garden, sharing its ever-changing moods: from
swirling torrent in the wetter months to a series of
quiet waterholes in summer.

Quince leaves floating on the pool.

Boy Cat lounging on the back terrace, getting some peace and quiet from the dogs.

A basket of quinces picked from the tree by the pool.

From a distance, the glow of the Manchurian pears can be seen through the cypresses.

An old copper basin, once used for washing clothes, now serves as the dogs' drinking bowl.

TOP LEFT Cypress trees and topiary balls stand around a cast Victorian fountain at the entrance. **TOP RIGHT** The house was constructed from the ruins of an old bluestone cottage. **BOTTOM LEFT** Ellouise. **BOTTOM RIGHT** English stone hounds guard the entrance to the main house.

The magnificent quince (*Cydonia oblonga*) in all its glory.

A row
of cypresses
planted in the
1860s.

Hedgerow Cottage

The cottage garden is brimful with flowering plants.

Hedgerow Cottage is
the quintessential Australian country
cottage and garden. Located in central Victoria,
the 1880s weatherboard is surrounded by a garden full
of surprises and delights—despite baking hot summers and
heavy winter frosts.

When John and Julie Mitchell bought the property eight years ago,
the cottage needed some love and attention, while the backyard was
an overgrown tangle of roses, clematis and the insidious arum lily (*Arum
italicum*)—not to mention buddleias as big as trees. During the laborious
clean-up, they uncovered the old dunny buried under a thicket—the outhouse
fallen to pieces around it, but the toilet itself standing proud in the middle of
the backyard.

Years of hard work have made huge changes. The garden is still full of lots
of remnant bulbs and self-sown treasures that pop up unannounced, but
now it feels well loved. Pushing open the picket gate, you walk up to
the house on a crunchy gravel path, surrounded by masses of plants.
Climbing roses run along the verandah and the garden beds are a tapestry
of cottage plants: clumps of iris, granny's bonnet (*Aquilegia*) and oriental
poppies. Carefree roses and clematis scramble up trees and into hedges.

Narrow paths snake between buxus topiary balls and pencil pines
(*Cupressus sempervirens*) to an area of raked granitic sand. There's a small,
perfectly kept lawn for the family's dogs, Miuccia and Maud, to play on.
Nearby is a bountiful vegetable garden, an old brick dairy (now used as a
toolshed) and a chook house. A pergola at the back of the house drips with
wisteria, roses and Chinese star jasmine (*Trachelospermum jasminoides*). There
is always something blooming in this garden, no matter what time of year
you visit.

Despite its recent resurrection, it feels like an old garden. The old
dunny and overgrown jungle of a backyard may be long gone, but the
original hawthorn hedge (*Crataegus monogyna*), after which the
cottage is named, is still there. With great sensitivity, Julie has
pruned, edited and revived different parts of the garden,
transforming it from an overgrown muddle to a very
romantic country cottage garden, a perfect
harmony of colour and texture.

Miuccia, beside an old stone trough that forms a water feature.

The garden at the front of the house is filled with roses, wisteria, aquilegias, irises and hundreds of different bulbs.

When John and Julie bought the property they could barely get out
the back door—they've transformed it into a flowering oasis.

Julie with Maude, the newest addition to the family.

TOP LEFT Miuccia enjoying Kyneton life. **TOP RIGHT** Honesty (*Lunaria annua*). **BOTTOM LEFT** Julie grows many varieties of iris. **BOTTOM RIGHT** Pink aquilegia (also known as granny's bonnet or columbine).

An addition at the back of the house blends with the existing building, draped with a climbing rose.

A climbing rose that was in the garden when Julie bought
the property has, under her care, come into its own.

Karkalla

The front garden at Karkalla with the 'tideline' running through.

In the front garden at
Karkalla, a tideline of smooth beach
glass, seashells and the odd shard of sea-
scoured pottery gives the appearance of having been
washed up by the ocean. Indeed, everything about this
Mornington Peninsula garden, owned by Fiona Brockhoff
and David Swann, reminds you that you are by
the sea.

Coastal rosemary (*Westringia fruticosa*), sea box (*Alyxia buxifolia*) and
Correa alba are clipped into waves and organic shapes that mimic the
nearby native bush that is sculpted by the salt-laden winds flying in
from Bass Strait, just a stone's throw away. Olive trees have been
pruned so that the canopies are high, allowing a clear view of the
ocean through the naked trunks. Phormium and spear grass
(*Austrostipa stipoides*) provide contrasting form and texture.

I remember seeing Karkalla for the first time, eighteen years
ago, and being blown away by the beauty and individuality of
Fiona's gardening and design style. Over the years, things have
changed in the garden—trees have grown, the odd plant has
been lost—but Karkalla maintains its unique spirit and personality.
The best gardens always show the hand and mind of the gardener
who created and maintains it, and it is clear that Fiona embraces
change and enjoys watching her garden evolve.

At Karkalla, the most commonplace peninsula natives become
stars, thanks to Fiona's clever clipping, editing and planting
combinations. The blend of native and exotic species creates
a garden that is always inspiring. It's a place you can visit
many times and still feel you have not seen it all—a
garden which leaves you wondering what more
riches yet remain to be discovered.

'The Thong Tree', made from flip-flops Fiona has
found washed up on the beach over the years.

Fiona working in the garden, the clipped shapes reminiscent of Japanese gardens.

The sculptural forms of the olive trees, their high canopies granting a clear view to the water.

TOP LEFT Fiona with Bonnie, her Jack Russell terrier. **TOP RIGHT** 1960s concrete garden pot with succulents. **BOTTOM LEFT** Fan aloe (*Kumara plicatilis*). **BOTTOM RIGHT** A specimen from Fiona's antique gnome collection.

The seating area in the back garden, featuring elegantly contoured clipped natives.

The once-bright limestone wall has mellowed with age. (When I first visited eighteen years ago, the walls were so dazzling you could hardly look at them.)

Copper water bowls placed throughout the garden attract birdlife.

Shona Nunan's striking bronze sculpture *The Journey* is the centrepiece of this garden.

Kate's Garden

Kate Herd is a woman
with many strings to her bow: artist,
author, landscape designer and passionate
gardener. Her own garden is in inner Melbourne, on
a stretch of the Yarra River. This might technically be a
city garden, but set on 2.4 hectares (6 acres), with borrowed
views of the bush along the river, to me it feels like a country
garden. The site slopes down from the house and the view out over
the garden is incredible; a textural tapestry of foliage rippling down
the hill. At the very bottom of the garden is a dam masquerading as a
natural billabong (this is where she gets the water to keep the garden
looking so lush).

Borders, terraces and granitic sand paths disguise the steep bank.
A diving accident at sixteen left Kate with a spinal cord injury,
so paths throughout the garden have been designed for easy
wheelchair access—although you will quite often find Kate
'bumming' (as she calls it) her way around as she weeds and plants.
As you wander along the winding tracks to the a large lawned area,
thick plantings obscure the house from view, creating a feeling of
complete immersion. The centrepiece of the lawn—and indeed
the garden—is a bronze sculpture, *The Journey* by Shona Nunan.
Exploring the garden, regular glimpses of bronze appear through
the greenery.

Kate has a distinct talent for including Australian natives in her
planting schemes, combining them with introduced species to
create her unique garden style. Kate has written a book called
Native with her best friend, Jela Ivankovic-Waters, which explores
the ways garden designers and creative people use native plants
in their work. Her own garden is a perfect balance of foliage
and flowers, texture and form. Kate is famous for her
saying, 'Gardening is my oxygen', and her garden is
testament to just how passionate she is.

The organic woven cubby house created by artist Gay Chatfield.

Kate has cleverly combined native and exotic plants throughout the garden. Here, mountain cabbage trees (*Cussonia paniculata*) have a strange prehistoric quality.

A view from the house over the garden, with the billabong and Yarra River in the background. The prehistoric-looking spiky seed heads belong to a giant honey flower (*Melianthus major*).

The cypress hedge at the top of the garden creates privacy, while raked granitic sand paths are designed to be wheelchair friendly.

Kate's dog, Inca: left, in real life; and right, in laser-cut steel.

Rusted-steel fencing blends with native grasses at the bottom of the garden.

TOP LEFT Pineapple lily (*Eucomis*). **TOP RIGHT** Native billy buttons (*Craspedia*).
BOTTOM LEFT Kangaroo paw (*Anigozanthos*) **BOTTOM RIGHT** *Euphorbia rigida*
and purple heart (*Tradescantia pallida*).

The gravel
motor court at
Killeen, planted with
leafy Chinese elms
(*Ulmus parvifolia*).

Killeen
Station

Killeen Station, in
the Strathbogie Ranges, is one of
Victoria's very first farming properties.
It was established in 1838, only three years after
Melbourne was settled. With 180 years of farming
history and well over 150 years of garden history, the
property is one of the most historically significant in the state.
The homestead and garden have evolved over time, with various
parts added and removed by shifting generations of residents and
owners, each keen to make their mark.

Today, the estate is owned by David and Joan Fowles, who bought
the place in 2003. They employed iconic landscape designer Rick
Eckersley to revitalise the garden, with the aim of linking the historic
plantings with newer parts of the garden to create a contemporary
interpretation. Both the house and garden—and even some of the
sheds and outbuildings—are listed by Heritage Victoria. Killeen
has significant early plantings, including the oldest wisteria vine
(*Wisteria sinensis*) recorded in Victoria and a white flowering cedar
(*Melia azedarach*) that is arguably the largest in the state. Also of
significance are three Irish strawberry trees (*Arbutus unedo*) and an
avenue of twenty-six Italian cypress (*Cupressus sempervirens*).

A dramatic entrance leads through to the homestead, the paved
area overarched by a large steel arbour covered with Boston ivy
(*Parthenocissus tricuspidata*), the vines hanging down in long tresses.
This part of Victoria can be very hot and dry, and shady plantings like
these are a clever way to create cool, breezy areas around the house.

Paths meander around the older trees and Rick has underplanted
here with masses of agave, euphorbia, kniphofia, limonium, day
lilies and melianthus major, to create a relaxed atmosphere.
Seamlessly combining the new with the old, Rick has given
Killeen a fresh new feel, producing a great country garden
that will hopefully live on for another 150 years.

The garden is a patch of green in the dry Australian landscape.

Rick has reinvigorated and reimagined the area around the historic white flowering cedar with his characteristic mass plantings. In the foreground are dramatic red-stemmed flower spikes of *Beschorneria septentrionalis*.

The extraordinary contrast between the green of the garden and the dusty landscape of Killeen Station.

TOP LEFT Ancient gums line the drive. **TOP RIGHT** The shearing shed.
BOTTOM The unusual red-brick stables have Flemish-style gable ends
built from bricks that were supposedly made on the property.

The ancient wisteria.

New plantings of *Melia azedarach* and yellow kniphofia complement the old flowering cedars.

Openings in the hedges create secret shortcuts between different parts of the garden.

The rose garden is one of Joan's favourite places to sit and relax.

Kylie Rose
Blake's Garden

Bright
vintage-style
sun lounges give
Kylie's garden a
resort feel.

Not every garden can
boast that it has a resident pig called
Percy, but Kylie Rose Blake's can. Percy has a
large run along one side of this garden in Scarsdale,
Victoria, and from his luxurious accommodation he enjoys
views of the garden and house on one side and bushland on the
other. It seems not a bad life!

Kylie designs gardens for a living, so it's fascinating to see what she's come
up with here, where she's had no brief other than to please herself. As you
enter the garden, the house is to one side, almost disappearing under a snarl
of climbing roses. To the other side of the driveway is a walled rose garden, its
moon-gate entrance inviting you in. Within are masses and masses of roses, each
one identified with a little recycled metal tag with a neatly written name. The rose
garden's walls are made from reclaimed sheets of corrugated iron—a nod to the
vernacular use of corrugated iron throughout the country—and the roses look
great against the rusty metal.

Kylie has used lots of other recycled bits and pieces in the garden to great
effect. In the front garden or 'Bubble Garden', amber glass balls catch the
late-afternoon light, glowing among plants clipped into spheres. Creating
a striking centrepiece is an installation of mosaic orbs and brightly painted
bamboo poles, emerging from some balls of coastal rosemary (*Westringia
fruticosa*). Various circular metal objects have been fixed to the garden fence,
continuing the theme of this part of the garden.

Vintage striped beach umbrellas and cane sun lounges in the seating areas
give a summer holiday feel to the garden and bring a smile to the face of
visitors. Repurposed items add an air of nostalgia throughout: antique teacups
and saucers filled with succulents are arranged in rows on pot-plant stands; old
olive oil tins are used to grow herbs and pelargoniums; even worn-out boots have
been given a new life as places to grow hardy plants.

Grapevines clamber up the verandah posts of the house Kylie built for herself.
Nearby is a chook house and a barbecue area with a wood-fired pizza oven.
In a quiet corner there's even an old-fashioned outdoor dunny. Raised beds
of clipped herbs and a vegetable garden with a countrified scarecrow
complete the garden. Kylie doesn't follow conventions, preferring to
do her own thing. Here she has created a beautiful, welcoming,
whimsical garden that perfectly reflects who she is.

The 'Bubble Garden'.

Kylie's cottage nestles amongst the roses.

The famous and handsome Percy the pig.

Kylie has saved a relic of Australian vernacular architecture.

Vintage finds and unusual objects in the garden.

The 'Bubble Garden' combines plant and sculptural elements, using lots of salvaged items.

The dam is a
beautiful element
of this garden, but in
the area's dry climate it's
also vitally important.
Lakithi is named after
the Zulu word for
'our home'.

Lakithi

From the moment
you enter the gates at Lakithi, it's
clear you're in for a garden treat. An avenue
of pin oaks (*Quercus palustris*), along with large
shrub and rambler roses, clematis and honeysuckle
(*Lonicera periclymenum*), line the driveway on the approach
to the house. Immediately, you can see the hand of a confident
gardener at work: generous borders filled with healthy-looking
plants and a beautifully kept lawn. The green thumb in this case
is Gail van Rooyen. Gail has used the site to full advantage, creating
considered views from the garden down to the dam and summerhouse
at the bottom of the hill, and out across paddocks strewn with bales of
cut hay. The result is a garden that feels generous and large.

Lakithi is very much a seasonal garden. In spring, the garden is full
of blossom, dogwoods and viburnum. A grove of silver birches
filled with thousands of bluebells (*Hyacinthoides non-scripta*)
has a romantic, European feel that seems a far cry from the often
harsh climate of Terip Terip in country Victoria. Clematis grows
madly and flowers profusely on structures throughout the garden,
scrambling up the verandah posts of the house. Summer sees the
roses reach full flight and Gail grows masses of them: the driveway
is a river of roses, while banks of rose bushes flank the summerhouse
and climbing varieties trail up the walls. Borders of perennial plants
come into their own, the foliage thick and flowers abundant.

The garden is a mix of formal and informal areas that flow together
seamlessly. A formal fountain area planted with *Viburnum tinus* hedges
and Washington thorn trees abuts a simple stone staircase planted
with French lavender (*Lavandula dentata*). The steps lead up to an
immaculate lawn at the front of the house, surrounded by wide
beds of perennials and shrubs. Here, and throughout the
garden, views of the surrounding farmland provide a
constant, peaceful background.

A lichen-covered bench beneath the branches of a Washington
thorn (*Crataegus phaenopyrum*) provides a shady place to sit.

TOP Robinia pseudocacia 'Frisia', underplanted with sweeps of sedum 'Autumn Joy', provides a splash of colour.
BOTTOM Stone steps bordered with lavender lead from the bottom of the garden up to the house.

TOP Gail is famous for her snowball trees (*Viburnum opulus*).
BOTTOM 'Double Purple' peony poppies (*Papaver somniferum*)
and *Calamagrostis* 'Karl Foerster' form a striking combination.

The first rays of morning sun catch the mist on the surface of the dam. The summerhouse, with its distinctive cone-shaped roof, can be seen behind.

Adirondack chairs for evening drinks by the dam.

Mass planting of sedum 'Autumn Joy' in the perennial borders at the front of the house.

Gail was given the seeds for this peony poppy by a friend.

TOP A spirea hedge (*Spiraea*) runs along the dam, creating colour in spring and summer. **BOTTOM LEFT** Gail in her four-wheel drive with Thombi (which means 'little girl' in Zulu). **BOTTOM RIGHT** A rowboat on the dam.

Morning-lit,
the silver birch
woodland, underplanted
with bluebells, is a
romantic corner of
the garden.

Lavandula

Early morning at Lavandula, with cypresses, lavender and more lavender.

Down a winding
country road is the atmosphere-laden
Lavandula, a lavender farm and garden owned
by Carol White. Inspired by her travels in the south
of France and Italy, Carol has created a slice of Provence in
central Victoria. She bought the 40-hectare (100-acre) property,
which includes an historic stone cottage and barn, in the late 1980s.
The house was built in the 1850s by Swiss-Italian settlers, the Tinettis,
who lived here with their thirteen children and were dairy farmers.

When Carol started gardening here she had no previous experience.
Through trial and error, she learnt what would grow in the area's harsh
climate—a mix of cold winters and hot, dry summers. She found that even
oleander (*Nerium oleander*), one of the toughest shrubs you can plant,
couldn't survive the bitter frosts. To help break the 'flow' of the frost
in winter, and to provide essential shade in summer, she has planted
rows of trees on the land around the gardens. She also feeds the soil
with mountains of sheep and poultry manure, and adds
dolemite lime.

A testament to Carol's dedication, the property today includes
avenues of trees, an olive grove, masses of fruit trees and shade
trees, and lots and lots of lavender. Medium and intermediate height
varieties of English lavender (*Lavandula angustifolia*) have been used, as
they produce the best amount of lavender oil—the farm now distils its
own oil to make lavender-based products.

A highlight of the year is the harvest festival, held in early January.
The lavender is hand cut with sickles, then bundled and hung to dry
on racks or under the airy verandah of the cottage. Some of the crop is
set aside to use in the still, which extracts the lavender oil. At harvest
time, the garden bustles with people enjoying market stalls and
live entertainment, eating and drinking at tables arranged
beneath the boughs of ash trees. This is a garden full of
trees, with many quiet shady spots to sit and take
in the views of the radiant purple fields and
the countryside beyond.

Café seating overlooks the fields of lavender.

Carol grows many species of lavender in the garden.

The stone barn makes it feel like you could be in rural France or Italy.

Rows of cypress trees add to the European atmosphere.

TOP A rose-covered arch forms a focal point among the lavender plantings.
BOTTOM The windmill is one of the few elements that reminds you that you're actually still in Australia.

Harvest time is the best time to visit.

A sea
of English
lavender.

Right by the beach, Luce Sulla Collina is a quirky mix of natives and exotics.

Luce Sulla Collina

This coastal garden on
the Great Ocean Road was created by
Melbourne landscape designer Kate Seddon.
The name of the property, Luce Sulla Collina, means
'light on the hill' in Italian. The garden is indeed on a steep
slope, which provided some interesting design challenges. In
addition, the house is built right on the back boundary, so there is
only a single area at the front of the block for the whole garden. Kate has
managed to cleverly incorporate the driveway, car parking and entertaining
areas into the space to create a relaxed, functional beach garden.

From the top of the garden, up by the road, a ribbon of blue water can be seen
above the roof of the house, hinting at the amazing panoramic views of the
Shipwreck Coast that can be enjoyed from inside. The generous path and steps
leading down through the garden are made from silvered aged timber and
look almost like the planks of an old jetty.

The lower part of the garden feels quite secluded, with planting on
the rock-walled bank providing privacy from the road. Large slabs of
bluestone pave the area outside the house, with native violets (*Viola
hederacea*), creeping thyme and seaside daisies (*Erigeron karvinskianus*)
softening the spaces between. A large weathered timber table in the
middle of the space matches the silvered cladding on the house.
When the owners are in residence, chairs are brought outside for casual
luncheons and dinners here, the garden functioning as an additional room
of the house. Four linden trees (*Tilia cordata*) shade the table in the warmer
months and their branches will eventually meet to create a natural umbrella
over the table.

Designed to need minimal maintenance (it's a beach house, after all), the
garden is a hardy mix of native plants and exotics, including many succulents.
Numerous custom elements add a warm personal touch. The beautiful house
name is chiseled into a large stone by the entry to the garden. Elsewhere,
a bowl carved into a block of bluestone forms a simple water feature
that attracts birds to the garden but also serves as a water bowl for
the family's dog. A slit cut into a gate at the side of the house
provides a keyhole view of the water: like so many other
aspects of this garden, it ensures you never forget
you're at the beach.

The weathered timbers of the house
complement the plantings of silver and grey.

All elements of the garden fit into the small space at the front of the house.

Existing native trees have been incorporated into the design.

The back of the house offers views of the ocean,
while the garden in front is completely self-contained.

A circular lawn with water views provides space for the dog to play.

TOP A custom-made water bowl cut from local stone.
BOTTOM LEFT The house name carved in stone.
BOTTOM RIGHT Weathered timber steps blend with the planting.

Deborah's garden has spilled out onto the nature strip and for a time was quite controversial in the area.

Melrose

It's difficult to believe
that in 2005 this house and garden in
Malmsbury, Victoria, were completely derelict.
Since buying Melrose just over a decade ago, Deborah
Hambleton and her partner, Rob van de Groenekan, have
created a fantastically productive garden that is literally
overflowing with life. The 1860s bluestone cottage has also been
restored and added to.

At the front of the house is a quite traditional rose garden, bulging at
the seams with roses and underplanted with cat mint, lambs ears and
other perennials, creating a space heady with colour and scent. Small
paths meander through the rest of the front garden, weaving between
pomegranate hedges and pencil pines. Within a hedged enclosure is the
swimming pool, surrounded by beds of lavender, miscanthus and fairy's
fishing rod (*Dierama pulcherrimum*). The plantings hug the pool so
tightly that indeed some offshoots flop into the water. An elegant
arbour made from bush poles (native saplings), with climbers
growing up it, creates dappled shade at one end of the
pool and provides a vertical element that gives the
garden scale and height. A rustic pool house sits
to one side, with walls made from railway sleepers
and a roof of rusted corrugated iron. Behind
the pool is a formal vegetable garden and a smart
chook house. Nearby there's an old building that was
the original kitchen, its location a reminder of the days
when wood stoves were a legitimate fire risk and thus built at
a distance from the main house.

The garden at Melrose is intensely cultivated and designed, every
square inch carefully considered and planned. Edible plants are a major
feature and the plants spilling over the front fence onto the verge
include herbs, medicinal plants, vegetables and fruit trees. Dwarf
quince, peach, cherry and Chilean guava trees, along with bay hedges
and more vegetables, fill a large section of the garden. More fruit
trees are scattered elsewhere, including pomegranate, goji berry,
nectarine and pistachio. Small step-over fruit trees, grafted
to dwarfing rootstock, have been planted against low
stone walls, so that even the most compact areas
of the garden are productive.

The area at the back of the house features two newly planted stone pines and a low-growing creeping eurphorbia (*E. cyparissias*).

The garden contains lots of special and rare things, including this handsome hound.

There's always a sheltered spot to sit and enjoy drinks in the garden, no matter what the weather is like.

Plantings around the pool house spill into the water.

A bush pole pergola covers the path to the pool house.

TOP Altissimo rose. BOTTOM LEFT A fountain in
the courtyard. BOTTOM RIGHT One of Deborah's
many collections of rare and unusual plants.

Rick's weekend cottage, nestled in amongst native trees.

Musk
Cottage

I am always interested
to see a landscape designer's own
garden, as it tends to be a place they experiment
and try out ideas—Rick Eckersley's garden is no
exception. Musk Cottage is located at tranquil Flinders on
the Mornington Peninsula. Rick purchased the 4-hectare (10-acre)
property in 2008 and set to work creating his ideal country escape: an
informal garden of soft lines and subdued colours. Gardens and art are
Rick's two big passions in life, and his eclectic sculpture collection adds an
element of humour to this otherwise serene garden. After almost twenty years
of spending Saturday mornings answering gardening questions on 3AW radio,
he now enjoys weekends in his garden.

The garden is not divided by formal hedges or plantings, but rather is made up
of two general zones: the lower part consists of a series of wetlands, dams and
gardens that rely on water; while the upper part is drier and more treed. The
massive curved timber deck attached to the house forms the epicentre;
from here you get great views down to the wetland areas and the many
paths curling off into the garden in all directions. The winding nature of
the tracks lends a softness to the space and there are so many that you can
tour the garden many times and never take the same route twice.

One of Rick's trademark design elements is his use of mass plantings:
why use one or two plants when you can use tens or, better still, hundreds!
Although the Musk Cottage garden features some succulents and exotics,
Rick has clearly indulged his passion for native plants. Repeated use of the
same eucalypt tree, or clumps of the same native grass, create a rhythm of
texture and colour.

This is a garden patently designed to be shared with friends and family.
There's comfortable seating on the central deck, where an eye-stopping
sculpture of a red man by Rick's nephew, Tom Eckersley, takes pride of
place. The dining area, under a pergola, is perfect for long lunches.
The pétanque court and swimming pool are relaxing places to while
away many a sunny afternoon. The pool area is perhaps the most
formal space in the garden: a dramatic gush of water cascading
from a height into the rectangle of dark water below.
However, a bordering mini-wetland of grasses and
aquatic plants prevents the area from
feeling too ordered.

Water-loving plants line the resort-style pool area.

The bottom part of the garden consists of wetlands that Rick has regenerated.

Rick's love of art and gardens coalesce at Musk Cottage.

The cottage and garden have been designed for relaxation and entertaining.

Overlooking the wetlands, the deck is the perfect spot for an evening drink.

Paths, like all the details in Rick's gardens, are highly considered and designed.   **Musk Cottage** / 219

TOP The sound of water falling into the pool is so relaxing.
BOTTOM Entertaining areas are incorporated into the garden design.

There are so many paths and each is different.

Natural bushland on the approach to Ray Brodie's Cottage.

Ray Brodie's Cottage

In the Adelaide Hills,
along a tree-lined gravel road that
looks to be straight out of a Hans Heysen
painting, is Ray Brodie's Cottage (named after the
man who built it). When Brenton and Libby Roberts bought
the 1860s cottage, on 2 hectares (5 acres), the house and garden
were in need of some serious love. Luckily, a challenge is just what
Brenton wanted. Six years of hard work later, the result is a relaxed,
productive country garden.

Brenton began by getting 600 tonnes of soil dumped in front of the house,
in order to create a flat lawn on what was a steeply sloping site. The house
no longer looks in danger of sliding down the hill and the kids have
somewhere to play. The rambling garden encircles the house and lawn.
Water is scarce here in summer and, although there is a bore, its use is
kept to a minimum. Thus the garden is planted with a mix of truly
hardy species such as sedums, miscanthus grasses, globe thistle
(*Echinops*), eryngium, wigandia, echiums and euphorbias. The area is
also prone to bushfires and the family's four goats—Mr Biggles, Gandalf
the Grey, Lowe and Snowy—do their bit to keep the undergrowth
under control.

Brenton has horticultural training and is no stranger to designing
gardens or propagating plants. He's expertly espaliered a fig tree to create
a living fence in front of the house, gently directing foot traffic along
the path and stopping garden visitors (and kids) from jumping from one
level of the garden to another. Manchurian pears (*Pyrus ussuriensis*) line
the driveway and will soon create a living tunnel as their branches begin
to entwine. Beneath the pears are 800 sedums, propagated by Brenton,
which create a fresh green approach to the house.

A kitchen garden near the back door of the house produces food
and herbs for the family. A fence of woven sticks and wire,
and a couple of beautiful rustic gates, protect the
produce from roving goats and keeps out the
odd kangaroo too.

To make forms like these, the topiary and espalier
processes must be started when the trees are very young.

Libby in the highly productive vegetable garden, behind a bush-twig fence.

Carefully considered details prove that even
a vegetable garden can be beautiful.

Sweet corn ready to be picked.

The fig trained along the stone wall forms a barrier between the lawn and the terrace, compelling two- and four-legged inhabitants to stick to the paths.

TOP The driveway is planted with Manchurian pears and sedums.
BOTTOM The original garden shed.

CLOCKWISE Brenton and Libby. The family dogs: Barry and Thorby. The family goats: Snowy and Lowe.

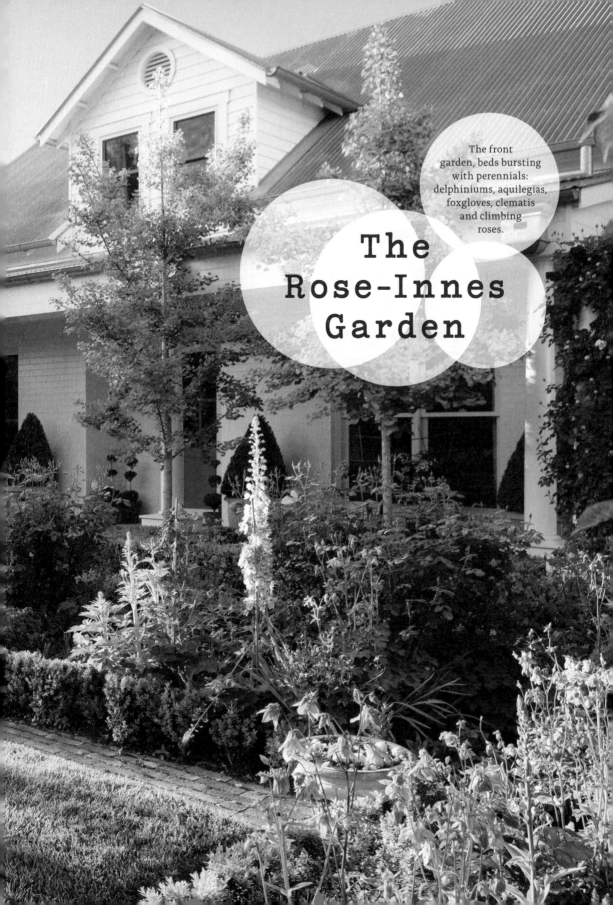

The front garden, beds bursting with perennials: delphiniums, aquilegias, foxgloves, clematis and climbing roses.

The Rose-Innes Garden

This garden in
Bowral, New South Wales,
belongs to passionate gardener and
author Jenny Rose-Innes and her husband,
Michael. Although this Southern Highlands garden
is only four years old, its seeming maturity shows just
what a clever gardener Jenny is. Bowral has the ideal climate
to grow plants, with rich soil and plenty of rain, but you need
a good eye and a green thumb to create something as impressive
as this. Both the new house and the garden look like they have
been there for many years, largely because Jenny, in her signature
style, has brought in many mature trees.

The garden has formal bones but a loose, romantic planting style.
The fresh green cones, balls and spirals of buxus topiary provide
an architectural framework, while climbing roses trail up fences
and perennial borders are bursting with interesting plant and
colour combinations. The front garden features a formal
rectangular pond and an arbour planted with roses.
An amazing faux bois table made by Victorian artist
Beau Johnstone is surrounded by beds crammed full
of perennials, with eye-popping splashes of intense blue
delphiniums, foxgloves and aquilegias.

From the back of the house you walk out onto a wide terrace,
with a seating area perfect for al fresco meals, afternoon drinks and
reading. A round brick-paved area with a large acanthus-leaf pot in
the middle is encircled by beds of silver-green and white plantings
and cones of clipped buxus. Across the neat green lawn (where
their dog, Penny, cavorts) is the most charming glasshouse you
will ever see; filled with plants, cuttings, germinating seeds
and neat rows of terracotta pots. Next door is Jenny's
studio and the potting bench where she spends
hours potting and re-potting the garden's
many pot plants and topiary.

Jenny's pride and joy is the custom-built glasshouse, where she
overwinters plants, sows seeds and propagates cuttings.

The garden in all its spring glory.

A seating area by the back door is showered with petals from the *Chionanthus virginicus* that shades the table in summer.

TOP LEFT Penny. **TOP RIGHT** The timber-framed windows of the glasshouse can be opened for ventilation on hot days. **BOTTOM LEFT** Plants on Jenny's potting bench. **BOTTOM RIGHT** An incredible Beau Johnstone faux bois table made from concrete.

The Rose-Innes Garden / 241

Garden beds bursting with spring growth.

The formal pond and timber rose arbour in the front garden.

A large French acanthus-leaf terracotta pot forms a striking
centre point in this area of the garden. The large ginko tree
in the background is a relic of the previous garden.

Rosebery Hill

Spring bluebells in full bloom under the old oak trees.

Tucked away in
the beautiful, rolling Macedon
Ranges is Rosebery Hill, the garden of
Barry and Ruth Murphy. Located in the hamlet
of Pipers Creek, the cosy cottage was originally Ruth's
grandfather's weekender and has been in the family since
the 1860s. Barry and Ruth share a passion for the unusual and
their garden contains many rare trees, shrubs and bulbs. It is a
garden full of atmosphere, a bit wild and romantic in places, with
fantastic old sheds and barns swallowed up by the greenery, and
beautiful vistas to the surrounding countryside.

The garden has a striking avenue of poplars that Barry has grown
from cuttings taken from old trees around Kyneton. Barry collects
oaks and has literally hundreds of different types. There are
numerous oak avenues: some featuring evergreens, others with
golden- or red-leaved varieties. The property has one of the
oldest and largest cork oaks (*Quercus suber*) in Australia:
the tree celebrates its 100th year in 2018.

The driveway up to the house is lined by a bewilderingly large
collection of daffodils—there are simply thousands of them, all
different sorts planted together and naturalised in a long, wide bed.
Large pompom-like camellias dot the driveway; at the start of spring
they are covered in so many blooms it can be hard to see any foliage.

Almost hidden, the 'main event' in this garden comes as a pleasant
surprise: an area of quirky topiary that Barry has been fostering for
some years now. After laboriously removing some dead Monterey
cypress trees (it took a couple of years to cut up the timber for
firewood!), he discovered some saplings had sprung up in their
place. He started clipping these and now the amazing array
of forms he's produced look like they have been there for
generations. Barry admits he's had some help from
gardener Mark, who assists with trimming
the larger topiary forms: 'He's tall and
a perfectionist,' laughs Barry.

Barry's eye-popping topiary is famous.

TOP The garden retains many of the original plantings, sheds and outbuildings. **BOTTOM** The garden is famous for its daffodils and is usually opened to the public for the local daffodil festival each spring.

TOP LEFT Barry and Ruth Murphy in the garden. **TOP RIGHT** Dougal.
BOTTOM LEFT Bluebells flowering under some of the old oaks. **BOTTOM
RIGHT** The fantastic topiary shapes are like a scene out of a Dr Seuss book.

The large, rambling garden is also a working farm.

TOP A couple of smaller clipped forms signal the entrance to the topiary garden. BOTTOM Barry says the camellias along the driveway do so well because they were grown from seed.

Daffodils
as far as the
eye can see.

Barry uses a three-legged topiary ladder to prune the taller forms.

The woodland garden at Shades of Gray.

Shades of Gray

At first glance, Peter
and Chelly Gray's garden seems to
be full of rare and unusual plants. Are those
stunning blue flowers over there under the birch
trees some rare meconopsis variety? But no, on closer
inspection, the blooms are in fact sculptures made with rusty
metal and wire. The garden, in Castlemaine in central Victoria,
is full of artworks created by Peter and Chelly. The artist couple run
a successful business, Shades of Gray, and the garden functions as an
outdoor gallery for their work, as well as a personal retreat.

The grounds include a renovated 1860s cottage, plus a studio and gallery,
and the garden is divided up into a number of different spaces. The front
of the cottage gets lots of sun and so is a great spot to grow succulents:
old concrete urns are filled with sedums and echeveria, which sprout
masses of pale-pink flowers. Chelly creates wire flowers to add
to the pots, making the plants into living works of art. The
house has an internal courtyard that houses a large metal
dining table made by Peter, overhung by a candle-filled
chandelier. Grapevines grow over a metal canopy
that is designed to keep the space cool in the
hot central Victorian summers.

In the middle of the garden is a small wooded
area of silver birch trees that creates shade and is
underplanted with ivy, violets and arum lilies. Larger
metal sculptures are displayed here, along with metal bird
houses, garden signs and swathes of metal flowers. The top of
the garden, meanwhile, houses the studio and gallery. Visitors
enter through antique metal gates, past a 2-metre tall arrangement
of luxuriant metal flowers.

Peter and Chelly hold an annual exhibition where they fill the
garden with all the art they have been working on. Each year their
work follows a different theme: animals, birds or plants. When
I visited, huge metal flowers were arranged throughout the
garden, pot plants were filled with smaller blooms, and
metal wreaths were scattered around. The entire
garden becomes a breathtaking art installation.

Coco Gray, Peter and Chelly's beloved hound.

Chelly creates stunning combinations of succulents and agaves that overflow from pots and containers.

TOP LEFT Coco greets visitors to the gallery and garden.
TOP RIGHT Steely the cat. **BOTTOM LEFT** Happy chooks.
BOTTOM RIGHT The luxurious hen house built by Peter
keeps the girls safe from foxes.

Along the side of the house is a pergola covered by a large rose. Ornate wirework chairs offer a quiet, shady spot to sit.

The cheery approach to the front door: old concrete urns filled
with masses of pink metal flowers and silver-leaved plants.

Decorative ceramic spheres adorn handmade frameworks for climbing roses and creepers.

Metal flowers bloom from every direction.

The courtyard at the back of the house offers a shady place to escape the summer heat.

Sunnymeade

A stunning *Cornus controversa variegata* in full flower.

On entering the
front gate of Sunnymeade, you feel
immediately transported to another place.
The property is located in the Strathbogie Ranges in
country Victoria, but you might just as well be in an English
garden planted a hundred years ago. Wide borders and generous
informal plantings greet you, inviting you to enter. On the driveway,
an intriguing stone building that looks like a little chapel draws you down
the path and further into the garden.

Sunnymeade is a large garden, conceived and built by Craig Irving with some
help from his parents, Margaret and John. Being virtually in the middle of nowhere,
Craig found it necessary to learn how to do everything himself—he has not only
planted and maintains the garden but has also built all of the structures. To his
credit, every element is meticulously crafted. A class on stone-wall building got
him started, and now the property has many stone walls and buildings, along
with a very beautiful moon gate.

The garden is divided into numerous 'rooms' that interconnect. Each room
has a different theme, so you never know what you will see next: perhaps a
Gothic building, a stone tower, a knot garden or a labyrinth path. Exploring the
garden, the viewer is cleverly drawn through the spaces by the placement of
eye-catching elements such as sculptures, mosaics, urns, arches and amazing
topiary. The use of space is also key, allowing the garden to reveal itself bit
by bit. Visitors pass through tiny rooms with high hedges, which lead on to
larger rooms filled with deep beds of lush perennials. Craig describes the garden
as 'a formal garden with informal planting', and that's exactly what it is.

Craig is a master of hedges. His hornbeam (*Carpinus betulus*) hedges are probably
the best you will ever see in Australia. 'Windows' in the hedges are so crisply cut
they could be carved from stone. In the afternoons, the openings allow shafts of
light to illuminate the plantings within. The whole garden feels so mature, with
its neat hedges and mellow stone walls, it's hard to believe that twenty years
ago it was just a paddock on the family farm.

Plantings here change with the seasons, so there is always something
in flower, whether peonies, clematis, dahlias, cyclamen, roses,
hollyhocks or foxgloves. In autumn, the changing leaves
provide masses of colour as the garden readies itself
for winter.

Peeking through one of the hedge windows to a formal pond surrounded by
plantings of hot-coloured dahlias and canna lilies in buxus-edged beds.

The Moorish garden: a blue garden pavilion and tiled central pond draw influence from gardens in Spain and North Africa.

The Gothic folly, built by Craig, is reflected in the formal circular pond.

TOP LEFT Craig with some of his spectacular topiary. **TOP RIGHT** Topiary guardians mark the entrance to yet another part of the garden. **BOTTOM LEFT** A labyrinth is set into the paving of this circular hedged room. **BOTTOM RIGHT** The laburnum walk in full flower. You can why it is often called the 'golden chain' or 'golden rain' tree.

Richly planted borders with *Muhlenbergia capillaris* (pink muhly grass), and topiary holly (*Ilex* 'Golden King') and golden bay tree. In the background is the golden autumn foliage of a variegated tulip tree (*Liriodendron tulipfera Aureo-marginatum*).

TOP The flawless parterre garden.
BOTTOM The hornbeam hedge surrounds a large terrace at the back of the house.

TOP The moon gate garden with beautiful rock walls, all built by Craig.
BOTTOM The little stone building just inside the entrance to the property
acts as a focal point and draws the visitor in to explore.

Sunlight
streams through
the eucalypts at
The Farmhouse.

The
Farmhouse

Halfway between
Kyneton and Daylesford, in the tiny
village of Denver, is Paul Bangay's country
residence, Stonefields. Right next door to the estate
is The Farmhouse, a low brick building that serves as
overflow accommodation for the main house and which
Paul also runs as a bed and breakfast. In my travels, I have
probably visited more Bangay gardens than anyone else, but the
deceptively simple garden that envelops The Farmhouse is one
of my all-time favourites. Vivid and textural, the garden embodies
Paul's love of colour and perennial plantings.

A stand of local eucalypts creates an understated backdrop for
the farmhouse and its garden. At the front of the house, three
wide beds surround a gravel court, each filled to overflowing
with colourful plantings. There are splashes of salvias,
phlomis, Russian sage, sedums and dahlias, and
clumps of smoke bush flaunt their bronzy
red foliage in the thickly planted borders.
With this bold design, Paul shows just what
a clever plantsman he can be when creating
for a very exacting client—in this case, himself.

The house itself sports a beautifully kept wisteria vine,
and clumps of box balls at the base of the verandah posts.
Tucked away down a country lane, The Farmhouse is only a
few hundred metres from Stonefields but the garden feels quite
private and has its own distinct, farmstead style.

Continuing a tradition started by the area's early settlers, Paul
has lined the laneway with hedges of hawthorn. At the rear
of the farmhouse, a wisteria-covered pergola provides a
shady spot to sit on summer evenings and admire the
backlit grasses, salvias and eupatorium.

Enormous eucalypts tower over the garden.

Smoke bush (*Cotinus coggygria*) adds its dark and dramatic foliage to the colourful perennial border.

Russian sage (*Perovskia atriplicifolia*) and coneflowers (*Rudbeckia*).

Mass plantings of Joe-Pye weed (*Eupatorium maculatum* 'Purpureum'),
carex grass, salvias and Russian sage.

Early morning light catches the lilac heads of Russian sage. In the foreground are dusky *Sedum telephium* 'Matrona' and rich violet *Salvia nemorosa*.

A seating area at the rear of the house is an ideal place to enjoy the garden and views to the countryside beyond.

Index

A vase of Meadowbank roses: one of each variety grown in the garden.

Acknowledgements

There are two very important things in my life: books and gardening. This book brings
them together and, I hope, shows the joy gardening brings. A day spent without getting your
hands in the soil or without reading books is a day wasted.

A big thank you to all the gardeners, friends and designers whose gardens are featured in the book.
Thank you for allowing me to photograph your gardens (often at odd times of the day), — it has
been a joy. Like gardens, people are all different, and that is part of what I love about photographing
gardeners and their gardens.

Thank you to my publisher, Kirsten Abbott, a garden lover who brought this book to life from a
tiny seed of an idea. And to the rest of the team at Thames & Hudson Australia for publishing
and believing in beautiful Australian books — may we always have gorgeous books in our lives.

To John Canty, a true gentleman of the design world, for his beautiful book design.
And to Jessica Redman, my editor extraordinaire, for her patience with me and my words.

More Information

Some of the gardens in the book are open to the public throughout the
year, while others are open to visitors under the Open Gardens Victoria
scheme or for local events.

Alowyn alowyngardens.com.au
Attila's Garden australiansucculents.com/events
Broughton Hall jindivickcountrygardener.com.au/broughton-hall
Cloudehill cloudehill.com.au
Flinders Garden benscott.com.au
Hedgerow Cottage kynetonbotanicgardensfriends.org/welcome
Luce Sulla Collina ksldesign.com.au
Karkalla fionabrockhoffdesign.com.au
Kate's Garden khaad.com.au
Killeen Station fowleswine.com/ourfarm
Kylie Rose Blake's Garden kylierose.gardens@bigpond.com
Lakithi opengardensvictoria.org.au
Lavandula lavandula.com.au
Melrose potagerdesigns.com.au
Musk Cottage e-ga.com.au
Ray Brodie's Cottage @brentonrobertsgardendesigns
Rosebery Hill kynetondaffodilarts.org.au
Shades of Gray shadesofgray.net.au
Sunnymeade sunnymeade.com.au
The Farmhouse stonefieldsthefarmhouse.com

First published in Australia in 2018
by Thames & Hudson Australia Pty Ltd
11 Central Boulevard Portside Business Park
Port Melbourne Victoria 3207
ABN: 72 004 751 964

thamesandhudson.com.au

ISBN: 978 1 7607600 8 3

 A catalogue record for this
book is available from the
National Library of Australia

Every effort has been made to trace accurate ownership of copyrighted text
and visual materials used in this book. Errors or omissions will be corrected
in subsequent editions, provided notification is sent to the publisher.

Design: John Canty
Editing: Jessica Redman
Printed and bound in China by RR Donnelley

FRONT COVER Berto at Meadowbank. **FRONT IMAGES** Manchurian pears and cypresses at Foss. Ian's studio at
Meadowbank. Dog, copper and *Nerium oleander* at Foss. The silver birch woodland at Broughton Hall. A Japanese maple at
Cloudehill. **REAR IMAGES** Peonies, grown in the garden at Foss. Rosebery Hill. **BACK COVER** Dahlias at Meadowbank.